THIS BOOK BELONGS TO:

NAME _____

SCHOOL _____

GRADE/SUBJECT _____

ROOM _____

SCHOOL YEAR _____

ADDRESS _____

PHONE _____

Authors: Darlene Spivak and Cynthia Holzschuher

Cover Art: Sue Fullam

Imaging: Ralph Olmedo, Jr.

Teacher Created Resources, Inc.
12621 Western Avenue
Garden Grove, CA 92841
www.teachercreated.com
ISBN: 978-1-57690-093-2
©1997 Teacher Created Resources, Inc.
Reprinted, 2017
Made in U.S.A.

TABLE OF CONTENTS

Ways to Use This Plan Book

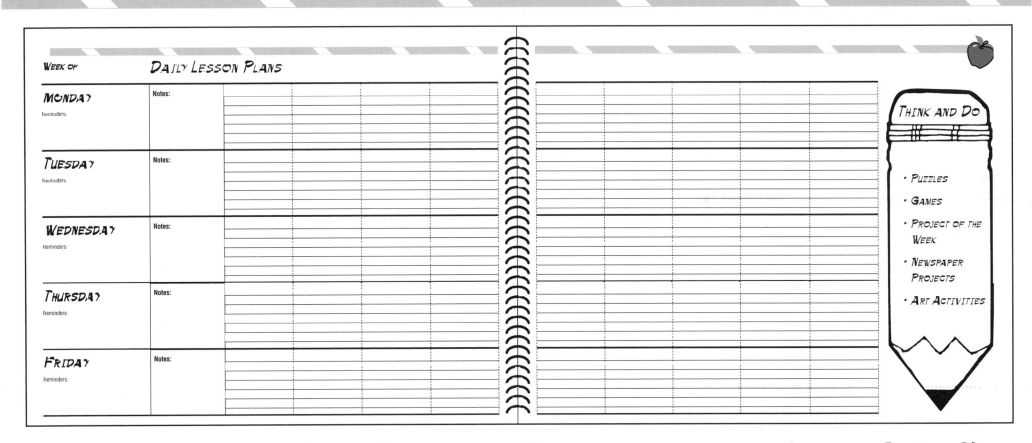

Seating Chart (page 3)

Table or desk arrangement will vary depending on room size, grade level, and actual teaching style preferred.

Suggestions have been given, but you may wish to customize your seating for the optimum learning benefits of your students.

Student Roster (pages 4 & 5)

Record both student and parent names and addresses. Make a special note of differences in last names when appropriate. You may wish to list siblings and their grades if they also attend your school. Notes may include special needs children and medications necessary.

Substitute Teacher Information (pages 6 & 7)

Record all pertinent information on these pages. If you have a copy of the layout of your school, attach it to this page; otherwise, sketch an outline of the school grounds, showing restrooms, office, lounge, playground, etc. Paper clip this page as well as the lesson plan page for easy reference.

Year at a Glance (page 8)

This section will give you an overview of the year and help focus on immediate and upcoming events, conferences, meetings, seminars, and other important dates. Record each event as soon as you are notified.

Birthdays (page 9)

Write names and birthdates of students in boxes. Identify each special day with a birthday greeting. With young children, sing to them and present them with a special birthday hat.

Emergency and First Aid Information (page 10)

Keep a First Aid Kit in an easy-to-find place and show the children where it is kept.

During the first week of school you may wish to go over the listed emergency information with your children.

In the blanks provided, list persons qualified to administer CPR along with their room numbers.

Literary Awards, Metric Conversions, Capital Cities, and World Map (pages 11–14)

These pages can be used as easy reference throughout the year. Also, you may wish to create puzzles and games using these fact pages.

Chalkboard Challenges (page 15)

These puzzles, games, and brain teasers will promote critical thinking for the students. They can be used as supplementary assignments, homework, or emergency substitute plans.

SEAT ARRANGEMENT IDEAS

Sticky notes can be used to temporarily assign seats.

1. Basic Row Seating

2. U-Shaped Seating

3. Rectangle   **4. Partner Seating**

The size and shape of your room will play a large part in your seating arrangement.

You may want to change this layout once you are familiar with your students and their needs.

Regardless of your seating plan, the most important concern is that you can easily see all your students and the children in turn have good visibility of you, the chalkboard, and other focal points in the room.

Front of Classroom

Student Roster

Student's Name	Parent's Name	Address	Home & Work Phones	Birthday	Siblings	Notes
1.						
2.						
3.						
4.						
5.						
6.						
7.						
8.						
9.						
10.						
11.						
12.						
13.						
14.						
15.						
16.						
17.						
18.						
19.						
20.						

STUDENT ROSTER

	Student's Name	Parent's Name	Address	Home & Work Phones	Birthday	Siblings	Notes
21.							
22.							
23.							
24.							
25.							
26.							
27.							
28.							
29.							
30.							
31.							
32.							
33.							
34.							
35.							
36.							
37.							
38.							
39.							
40.							

Substitute Teacher Information

School Schedule

- Class Begins _____
- Morning Recess _____
- Lunchtime _____
- Class Resumes _____
- Afternoon Recess _____
- Dismissal _____

Special Notes

Special Classes

Student _____Class _____Day _____Time _____

Student _____Class _____Day _____Time _____

Student _____Class _____Day _____Time _____

Special Needs Students

Student	Needs	Time and Place
_____	_____	_____
_____	_____	_____
_____	_____	_____
_____	_____	_____
_____	_____	_____

Where to Find

- Class List _____
- School Layout_____
- Seating Chart _____
- Attendance Record _____
- Lesson Plans _____
- Teacher Manuals_____
- First Aid Kit_____
- Emergency Information _____
- Supplementary Activities _____
- Class Supplies–paper, pencils, etc _____
- Referral forms and procedures_____

_____

_____

_____

_____

_____

_____

_____

_____

_____

_____

_____

_____

_____

_____

CLASSROOM STANDARDS

- When finished with an assignment

  _____

  _____

- When and how to speak out in class

  _____

  _____

- Incentive Program

  _____

  _____

- Discipline

  _____

  _____

- Restroom Procedure

  _____

  _____

PEOPLE WHO CAN HELP

- Teacher/Room _____
- Dependable Students _____

  _____

  _____

  _____

  _____

- Principal _____
- Secretary _____
- Custodian _____
- Counselor _____
- Nurse _____

LAYOUT OF SCHOOL—including school office, teachers' lounge, restrooms, auditorium, playground, etc. (or attach printed diagram here)

YEAR AT A GLANCE

August	September	October	November

December	January	February	March

April	May	June	July

BIRTHDAYS

August	September	October	November

December	January	February	March

April	May	June	July

EMERGENCY AND FIRST AID INFORMATION

CLASSROOM CAUTION

- Do not move a person who is seriously injured.
- Report all head injuries to the nurse or office.
- Show children where the first aid kit is stored.
- List students with medical problems and any medications.
- Instruct children about nose blowing and covering their mouths when coughing and sneezing.
- Inform students about what to do if they feel they are going to be ill.
- The best way to stop bleeding is to put pressure on the wound.

  a. Use a clean pad, a cloth, a plastic bag, or any other object that will keep you from touching the blood directly. (Never allow the blood to touch your skin.)

  b. Place your hand over the pad or cloth, pressing firmly and steadily until the bleeding stops or someone comes to help.

  c. Do not remove the pad or cloth. You might start the bleeding again. Instead, add more pads or cloth and keep pressing.

  d. If the part that is bleeding can be raised higher than the victim's head, do so; this will slow down the flow of blood.

  e. Keep the victim from moving—especially the wounded area.

EMERGENCY DRILL PROCEDURES

FIRST AID FOR CHOKING
Adults/Children

If conscious but *choking*...

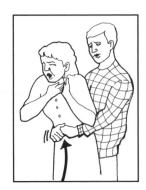

Give abdominal thrusts until object comes out.

If person becomes *unconscious*...

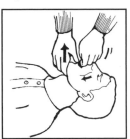

Step 1
Clear any object from the mouth.

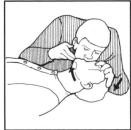

Step 2
Give two slow breaths.

If air won't go in...

Step 3
Give up to five abdominal thrusts.

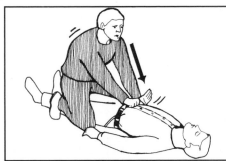

Repeat steps 1, 2, & 3 until breaths go in or help arrives.

TRAINED CPR PERSON AT OUR SCHOOL:

Name _____ Room _____

Name _____ Room _____

Name _____ Room _____

The Newbery Medal is awarded each year to the author of the most distinguished contribution to children's literature published in the United States. Here are the winners from 1965 to 2005.

Year Title/Author

2007 *The Higher Power of Lucky.* Susan Patron
2006 *Criss Cross.* Lynne Rae Perkins
2005 *Kira-Kira.* Cynthia Kadohata
2004 *The Tale of Despereaux.* Kate DiCamillo
2003 *Crispin: The Cross of Lead.* Avi
2002 *A Single Shard.* Linda Sue Park
2001 *A Year Down Yonder.* Richard Peck
2000 *Bud, Not Buddy.* Christopher Paul Curtis
1999 *Holes.* Louis Sachar
1998 *Out of The Dust.* Karen Hesse
1997 *The View From Saturday.* E.L. Konigsburg
1996 *Midwife's Apprentice.* Karen Cushman
1995 *Walk Two Moons.* Sharon Creech
1994 *The Giver.* Lois Lowry
1993 *Missing May.* Cynthia Rylant
1992 *Shiloh.* Phyllis Reynolds
1991 *Maniac Magee.* Jerry Spinelli
1990 *Number the Stars.* Lois Lowry
1989 *Joyful Noise.* Paul Fleischman
1988 *Lincoln: A Photobiography.* Russell Freedman
1987 *The Whipping Boy.* Sid Fleischman
1986 *Sarah, Plain and Tall.* Patricia MacLachlan
1985 *The Hero and the Crown.* Robin McKinly
1984 *Dear Mr. Henshaw.* Beverly Cleary
1983 *Dicey's Song.* Cynthia Voigt
1982 *A Visit to William Blake's Inn.* Nancy Willard
1981 *Jacob Have I Loved.* Katherine Paterson
1980 *A Gathering of Days.* Joan W. Blos
1979 *The Westing Game.* Ellen Raskin
1978 *Bridge to Terabithia.* Katherine Paterson
1977 *Roll of Thunder, Hear My Cry.* Mildred Taylor
1976 *The Grey King.* Susan Cooper
1975 *M.C. Higgins, the Great.* Virginia Hamilton
1974 *The Slave Dancer.* Paula Fox
1973 *Julie of the Wolves.* Jean George
1972 *Mrs. Frisby and the Rats of NIMH.* Robert C. O'Brien
1971 *Summer of the Swans.* Betsy Byars
1970 *Sounder.* William H. Armstrong
1969 *The High King.* Lloyd Alexander
1968 *From the Mixed-Up Files of Mrs. Basil E. Frankweiler.* Elaine Konigsburg
1967 *Up a Road Slowly.* Irene Hunt
1966 *I, Juan de Pareja.* Elizabeth Borton de Trevino
1965 *Shadow of a Bull.* Maia Wojciechowska

The Caldecott Medal is presented to the illustrator of the most distinguished picture book for children published in the United States. Here are the winners from 1965 to 2005.

Year Title/Illustrator

2007 *Flotsam.* David Wiesner
2006 *The Hello, Goodbye Window.* Chris Raschka
2005 *Kitten's First Full Moon.* Kevin Henkes
2004 *The Man Who Walked Between the Towers.* Mordicai Gerstein
2003 *My Friend Rabbit.* Eric Rohmann
2002 *The Three Pigs.* David Wiesner
2001 *So You Want to Be President?* Illustrated by David Small; text by Judith St, George
2000 *Joseph Had a Little Overcoat.* Simms Taback
1999 *Snowflake Bentley.* Illustrated by Mary Azarian; text by Jacqueline Briggs Martin
1998 *Rapunzel.* Paul O. Zelinsky
1997 *Golem.* David Wishiewski
1996 *Officer Buckle and Gloria.* P. Rathmann
1995 *Smoky Night.* David Diaz
1994 *Grandfather's Journey.* Allen Say
1993 *Mirette on the High Wire.* Emily A. McCully
1992 *Tuesday.* David Wiesner
1991 *Black and White.* David Macaulay
1990 *Lon Po Po.* Ed Young
1989 *Song and Dance Man.* Stephen Gammell
1988 *Owl Moon.* John Schoenherr
1987 *Hey, Al.* Richard Egielski
1986 *The Polar Express.* Chris Van Allsburg
1985 *Saint George and the Dragon.* Trina Schart Hyman
1984 *The Glorious Flight: Across the Channel with Louis Bleriot.* Alice and Martin Provensen
1983 *Shadow.* Marcia Brown
1982 *Jumanji.* Chris Van Allsburg
1981 *Fables.* Arnold Lobel
1980 *Ox-Cart Man.* Barbara Cooney
1979 *The Girl Who Loved Wild Horses.* Paul Goble
1978 *Noah's Ark.* Peter Spier
1977 *Ashanti to Zulu: African Traditions.* Leo and Diane Dillon
1976 *Why Mosquitoes Buzz in People's Ears.* Leo and Diane Dillon
1975 *Arrow to the Sun: A Pueblo Indian Tale.* Gerald Mc Dermott
1974 *Duffy and the Devil.* Margot Zemach
1973 *The Funny Little Woman.* Blair Lent
1972 *One Fine Day.* Nonny Hogrogian
1971 *A Story, A Story.* Gail E. Haley
1970 *Sylvester and the Magic Pebble.* William Steig
1969 *The Fool of the World and the Flying Ship.* Uri Shulevitz
1968 *Drummer Hoff.* Ed Emberley
1967 *Sam, Bangs and Moonshine.* Evaline Ness
1966 *Always Room for One More.* Nonny Hogrogian
1965 *May I Bring a Friend?* Beni Montresor

METRIC CONVERSIONS

LINEAR

100 cm	=	1 meter
cm	=	centimeter
$\frac{1}{4}$"	=	.6 cm
$\frac{1}{2}$"	=	1.3 cm
1"	=	2.54 cm
3"	=	7.62 cm
6"	=	15.24 cm
9"	=	22.86 cm
12"	=	30.48 cm
18"	=	45.72 cm
24"	=	61 cm
36"	=	91.44 cm
100 yds	=	91.4 m
1 mile	=	1,609 m

VOLUME (DRY AND LIQUID)

L	=	liter
mL	=	milliliter = .001 L
1 tsp	=	5 mL
1 T	=	15 mL
$\frac{1}{4}$ c	=	59 mL
$\frac{1}{2}$ c	=	118 mL
1 c	=	236 mL or 8 oz. = .236 L
1 oz	=	30 mL
1 pt	=	about .5 L (473.2 mL)
1 qt	=	about 1 L (946.4 mL)
1 gal	=	about 3.8 L
1 L	=	1.0567 qts liquid
1 qt dry	=	1.101 L
1 qt liquid	=	.09463 L
1 gal liquid	=	3.78541 L

TEMPERATURES

To convert Fahrenheit to Celsius (F° - 32 x .55)
To convert Celsius to Fahrenheit (C° x 1.8) + 32

	Celsius	Fahrenheit
Boiling Point of Water	100°	212°
Freezing Point of Water	0°	32°
Cold Day	-20°	-4°
Room Temperature	20°	66°
Body Temperature	37°	98.6°

Oven Temperatures

	Celsius	Fahrenheit
warm oven	135°	275°
moderate oven	175°	350°
hot oven	204°	400°

WEIGHTS

1 gram	=	0.03527 ounce
1 ounce	=	28.35 gram
1 kilogram	=	2.2046 lbs
1 pound	=	453.4 gram or .454 kilogram
1 ton	=	908 kilograms

STATES AND CAPITALS

UNITED STATES

State	Capital	State	Capital	State	Capital
Alabama	Montgomery	Louisiana	Baton Rouge	Ohio	Columbus
Alaska	Juneau	Maine	Augusta	Oklahoma	Oklahoma City
Arizona	Phoenix	Maryland	Annapolis	Oregon	Salem
Arkansas	Little Rock	Massachusetts	Boston	Pennsylvania	Harrisburg
California	Sacramento	Michigan	Lansing	Rhode Island	Providence
Colorado	Denver	Minnesota	St. Paul	South Carolina	Columbia
Connecticut	Hartford	Mississippi	Jackson	South Dakota	Pierre
Delaware	Dover	Missouri	Jefferson City	Tennessee	Nashville
Florida	Tallahassee	Montana	Helena	Texas	Austin
Georgia	Atlanta	Nebraska	Lincoln	Utah	Salt Lake City
Hawaii	Honolulu	Nevada	Carson City	Vermont	Montpelier
Idaho	Boise	New Hampshire	Concord	Virginia	Richmond
Illinois	Springfield	New Jersey	Trenton	Washington	Olympia
Indiana	Indianapolis	New Mexico	Santa Fe	West Virginia	Charleston
Iowa	Des Moines	New York	Albany	Wisconsin	Madison
Kansas	Topeka	North Carolina	Raleigh	Wyoming	Cheyenne
Kentucky	Frankfort	North Dakota	Bismarck		
				Nation's Capital	Washington, D.C.

CANADA

Province	Capital
Alberta	Edmonton
British Columbia	Victoria
Manitoba	Winnipeg
New Brunswick	Fredericton
Newfoundland	St. John's
Nova Scotia	Halifax
Ontario	Toronto
Prince Edward Island	Charlottetown
Quebec	Quebec
Saskatchewan	Regina

Territories

Northwest Territories	Yellowknife
Yukon Territory	Whitehorse

MEXICO

State	Capital	State	Capital
Aguascalientes	Aguascalientes	Morelos	Cuernavaca
Baja California Norte	Mexicali	Nayarit	Tepic
Baja California Sur	La Paz	Nuevo León	Monterrey
Campeche	Campeche	Oaxaca	Oaxaca
Chiapas	Tuxtla Gutierrez	Puebla	Puebla
Chihuahua	Chihuahua	Querétaro	Querétaro
Coahuila	Saltillo	Quintana Roo	Chetumal
Colima	Colima	San Luis Potosí	San Luis Potosí
Durango	Durango	Sinaloa	Culiacán
Federal District	—	Sonora	Hermosillo
Guanajuato	Guanajuato	Tabasco	Villahermosa
Guerrero	Chilpancingo	Tamaulipas	Ciudad Victoria
Hidalgo	Pachuca	Tlaxcala	Tlaxcala
Jalisco	Guadalajara	Veracruz	Jalapa
México	Toluca	Yucatán	Mérida
Michoacán	Morelia	Zacatecas	Zacatecas

WORLD MAP

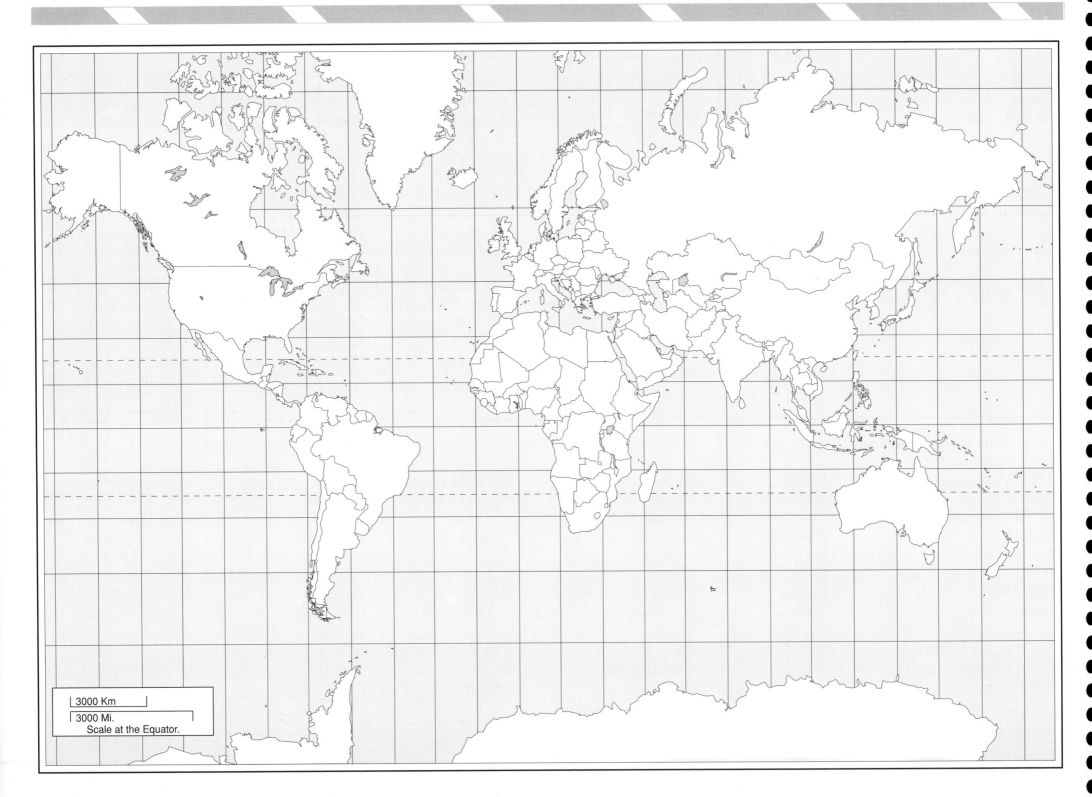

3000 Km
3000 Mi.
Scale at the Equator.

CHALKBOARD CHALLENGES

These challenges can be easily written on the chalkboard for students to work on as assignments or in their free time.

1. List as many items as you can that are sold in pairs.

2. Make a list of words that have five vowels within them.

3. List words related to fall, winter, spring, and summer that begin with each letter of the alphabet.

Use the Value Box below and have students find the values of various words, holiday sayings, etc. Example: The word *school* is worth $72.
(19+3+8+15+15+12 = 72)

4. Name as many things as you can that have holes.

5. List food items that begin with each letter of the alphabet from A–Z.

6. Draw a picture of a farm with 2 cows, 6 ducks, 3 pigs, 4 sheep and 1 farmer.

7. Write a word that begins with **a** and ends with **b**; begins with a **b** and ends with **c**; begins with **c** and ends with **d**; and so on through the alphabet.

8. Write four words that rhyme with *goat—pick—true—tie—stamp—line—free—plan—sad—meet—hop—dog—sun.*

9. List the opposites of *friend—tall—boy—good—early—loud—young—large—low— hard—dark—down—dry—out—fast.*

10. Name something: green, furry, slow, shiny, strange, pretty, purple, sweet, big, curly, yellow.

11. Write words from A–Z that begin and end with the same letter.

12. Make a list of words that contain two of each letter (example: 2 a's–**a**lw**a**ys).

Value Box

A=	$1	O=	$15
B=	$2	P=	$16
C=	$3	Q=	$17
D=	$4	R=	$18
E=	$5	S=	$19
F=	$6	T=	$20
G=	$7	U=	$21
H=	$8	V=	$22
I=	$9	W=	$23
J=	$10	X=	$24
K=	$11	Y=	$25
L=	$12	Z=	$26
M=	$13		
N=	$14		

WEEK OF _____ DAILY LESSON PLANS

MONDAY Reminders:_____ _____ _____	Notes:				
TUESDAY Reminders:_____ _____ _____	Notes:				
WEDNESDAY Reminders:_____ _____ _____	Notes:				
THURSDAY Reminders:_____ _____ _____	Notes:				
FRIDAY Reminders:_____ _____ _____	Notes:				

THINK AND DO

- PUZZLES
- GAMES
- PROJECT OF THE WEEK
- NEWSPAPER PROJECTS
- ART ACTIVITIES

DAILY LESSON PLANS

MONDAY					
Reminders: _____	Notes:				
_____					
_____					

TUESDAY					
Reminders: _____	Notes:				
_____					
_____					

WEDNESDAY					
Reminders: _____	Notes:				
_____					
_____					

THURSDAY					
Reminders: _____	Notes:				
_____					
_____					

FRIDAY					
Reminders: _____	Notes:				
_____					
_____					

THINK AND DO

Challenge your students to create a code by assigning a different number to each letter of the alphabet. They should use the code to write simple messages that can be traded and decoded by their friends at some point during the school day. Students may also write the lunch menu or a familiar nursery rhyme in a code. Assign a number (0-9) to each letter of the alphabet. Each morning, ask students to add the numbers of letters that spell the day. Keep a running total and, on Friday, add the five daily numbers to get a weekly total. You may do the same with the months of the year or a list of names.

DAILY LESSON PLANS

MONDAY

Reminders: _____

_____

_____

Notes:

TUESDAY

Reminders: _____

_____

_____

Notes:

WEDNESDAY

Reminders: _____

_____

_____

Notes:

THURSDAY

Reminders: _____

_____

_____

Notes:

FRIDAY

Reminders: _____

_____

_____

Notes:

THINK AND DO

Provide several telephone books for your students to use in searching for last names that are color words or animal names. Draw a picture of one person that gives a clue to his or her name.

Another day, students may do a similar search for last names that are nouns or verbs. The telephone book is the source of valuable information about local hospitals, libraries, businesses, zip codes, and maps. Each day write two locations for which students are to supply phone numbers. They may also use the perpetual calendar (if one is included) to determine the day of important historical events (like July 4, 1776).

DAILY LESSON PLANS

MONDAY					
Reminders: _____ _____ _____	Notes:				

TUESDAY					
Reminders: _____ _____ _____	Notes:				

WEDNESDAY					
Reminders: _____ _____ _____	Notes:				

THURSDAY					
Reminders: _____ _____ _____	Notes:				

FRIDAY					
Reminders: _____ _____ _____	Notes:				

THINK AND DO

Ask each student to keep a food diary of a day and classify the items according to basic food groups (grain, fruit/vegetables, milk/cheese, and meat). Be sure to point out that some items may contain foods from several different groups (tacos, pizza, etc.).

Later, collect the diaries and use the information to determine the students' favorite foods, as well as dietary shortcomings. Explain the food pyramid and encourage your students to make wise choices. Create original recipes, using favorite healthful foods. Send the recipes home and encourage your students to prepare samples of taste tests.

WEEK OF _____ # DAILY LESSON PLANS

MONDAY

Reminders:_____

_____

_____

Notes:

TUESDAY

Reminders:_____

_____

_____

Notes:

WEDNESDAY

Reminders:_____

_____

_____

Notes:

THURSDAY

Reminders:_____

_____

_____

Notes:

FRIDAY

Reminders:_____

_____

_____

Notes:

THINK AND DO

Have students make a story map, showing the sequence of events and/or locations for any picture or chapter book. They will need a large sheet of white roll paper. As a group, students will decide on a list of events they will include. Have students make a series of pictures to represent them. Pictures should be joined with arrows to make a path from beginning to end. Number the pictures in order. If appropriate, write a sentence near each one. Use the map in retelling the story to another class. Other students may wish to use the list of events (or scenes) to create dioramas and write paragraphs explaining each one. Display them in story order.

DAILY LESSON PLANS

MONDAY

Reminders:_____

_____

_____

Notes:

TUESDAY

Reminders:_____

_____

_____

Notes:

WEDNESDAY

Reminders:_____

_____

_____

Notes:

THURSDAY

Reminders:_____

_____

_____

Notes:

FRIDAY

Reminders:_____

_____

_____

Notes:

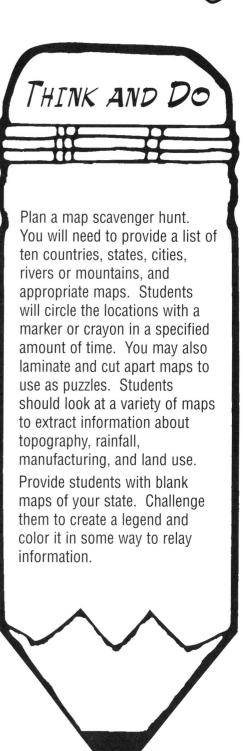

THINK AND DO

Plan a map scavenger hunt. You will need to provide a list of ten countries, states, cities, rivers or mountains, and appropriate maps. Students will circle the locations with a marker or crayon in a specified amount of time. You may also laminate and cut apart maps to use as puzzles. Students should look at a variety of maps to extract information about topography, rainfall, manufacturing, and land use.

Provide students with blank maps of your state. Challenge them to create a legend and color it in some way to relay information.

MONDAY

Reminders:_____

_____

_____

Notes:

TUESDAY

Reminders:_____

_____

_____

Notes:

WEDNESDAY

Reminders:_____

_____

_____

Notes:

THURSDAY

Reminders:_____

_____

_____

Notes:

FRIDAY

Reminders:_____

_____

_____

Notes:

THINK AND DO

Choose different students to chart the outside temperature at the same time each day. Use this information to compute a weekly average. On Friday, use the newspaper to compare the class's temperatures with those of another city. Have students list cities that have higher, lower, and similar readings.

Discuss/write: Would you prefer to live in a warmer or colder climate? What is positive or negative about the weather where you live? Is your mood or behavior affected by the weather? How should you dress for each type of weather? If possible, invite a meteorologist to visit your class. Make a list of questions that you would like to ask.

WEEK OF _____ *DAILY LESSON PLANS*

MONDAY Reminders: _____ _____ _____	Notes:			
TUESDAY Reminders: _____ _____ _____	Notes:			
WEDNESDAY Reminders: _____ _____ _____	Notes:			
THURSDAY Reminders: _____ _____ _____	Notes:			
FRIDAY Reminders: _____ _____ _____	Notes:			

THINK AND DO

Home—Have students ask their parents on what day of the week they were born. Bring the information to class and make a bar graph.

Have students write a story describing a perfect birthday. Share the poem "A Week of Birthdays" (Mother Goose). Ask each student to draw a self-portrait that indicates an understanding of the poem. Be sure that all your students can say the days of the week in order and know their abbreviations.

As a group, brainstorm a daily list of special events for the current week (include TV shows, games, shopping trips, etc.). Students should include this information in a personal writing journal.

WEEK OF _____ # DAILY LESSON PLANS

MONDAY

Reminders:_____

_____

_____

Notes:

TUESDAY

Reminders:_____

_____

_____

Notes:

WEDNESDAY

Reminders:_____

_____

_____

Notes:

THURSDAY

Reminders:_____

_____

_____

Notes:

FRIDAY

Reminders:_____

_____

_____

Notes:

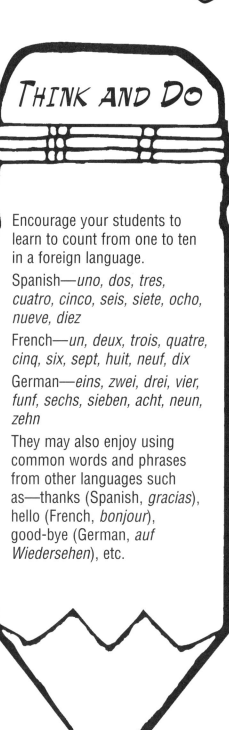

THINK AND DO

Encourage your students to learn to count from one to ten in a foreign language.

Spanish—*uno, dos, tres, cuatro, cinco, seis, siete, ocho, nueve, diez*

French—*un, deux, trois, quatre, cinq, six, sept, huit, neuf, dix*

German—*eins, zwei, drei, vier, funf, sechs, sieben, acht, neun, zehn*

They may also enjoy using common words and phrases from other languages such as—thanks (Spanish, *gracias*), hello (French, *bonjour*), good-bye (German, *auf Wiedersehen*), etc.

DAILY LESSON PLANS

MONDAY

Reminders:_____

_____

_____

Notes:				

TUESDAY

Reminders:_____

_____

_____

Notes:				

WEDNESDAY

Reminders:_____

_____

_____

Notes:				

THURSDAY

Reminders:_____

_____

_____

Notes:				

FRIDAY

Reminders:_____

_____

_____

Notes:				

THINK AND DO

Home—Ask each student to bring in a baby picture. Assign each picture a number and post them on a bulletin board. Provide a numbered fill-in sheet for students to try to guess who's who. You may wish to plan a similar activity using several teachers' baby pictures. Discuss with your students how people change over time. Assign each student to write an autobiography from birth that projects into the future to adulthood. Design birth certificates showing full name and birthdate.

DAILY LESSON PLANS

MONDAY Reminders:_____ _____ _____	Notes:			
TUESDAY Reminders:_____ _____ _____	Notes:			
WEDNESDAY Reminders:_____ _____ _____	Notes:			
THURSDAY Reminders:_____ _____ _____	Notes:			
FRIDAY Reminders:_____ _____ _____	Notes:			

THINK AND DO

Distribute newspapers and highlighters and ask students to mark any of the following: compound words, double letters or numbers, spelling words, the letters of their names, color/number words, etc., in a specified amount of time.

Another day, cut apart cartoon strips and ask able students to glue them in order to another paper.

You may also ask students to circle the *who, what, where, when,* and *why* facts in a typical news article. Examine advertisements for information in a brief format.

MONDAY

Reminders:_____

_____

_____

Notes:

TUESDAY

Reminders:_____

_____

_____

Notes:

WEDNESDAY

Reminders:_____

_____

_____

Notes:

THURSDAY

Reminders:_____

_____

_____

Notes:

FRIDAY

Reminders:_____

_____

_____

Notes:

THINK AND DO

Have each student write or call the 1-800 number of the tourism bureau for the state of your choice. Request information on points of interest. Later, the results can be shared through displays and/or reports. Students can mark each location on a map of the United States. Invite students to vote for the best vacation spot. Determine its distance from their hometowns and contact a travel agency to plan a dream trip. Teach related vocabulary: *resort, amusement park, national park, monument, campground,* etc., and compile a class book of national vacation spots.

WEEK OF _____ DAILY LESSON PLANS

MONDAY

Reminders: _____

_____

_____

Notes:

TUESDAY

Reminders: _____

_____

_____

Notes:

WEDNESDAY

Reminders: _____

_____

_____

Notes:

THURSDAY

Reminders: _____

_____

_____

Notes:

FRIDAY

Reminders: _____

_____

_____

Notes:

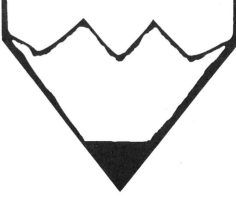

THINK AND DO

Brainstorm with students a list of cold cereals. Put them in ABC order. Classify them by grain (wheat, corn, oats, mixed). List adjectives that describe the taste and appearance of each cereal. Survey several students in another class to determine the top five cereal choices. Graph the results. Have a cold cereal snack. Collect empty cereal boxes and coupons to use for matching activities. Print prices on the packages and ask older students to match and subtract the coupon value. Use letter-shaped cereals for spelling practice.

DAILY LESSON PLANS

MONDAY

Reminders:_____

_____

_____

Notes:

TUESDAY

Reminders:_____

_____

_____

Notes:

WEDNESDAY

Reminders:_____

_____

_____

Notes:

THURSDAY

Reminders:_____

_____

_____

Notes:

FRIDAY

Reminders:_____

_____

_____

Notes:

THINK AND DO

Have students make this story wind sock. Have students choose their favorite character from a book. Then have them draw, color, and cut out their own pictures of the characters. Cut the top and bottom from a clear two-liter soda bottle. Glue story characters onto the outside of the plastic cylinder. Write 6–8 sentences about the story on strips of colored paper. Staple them in place at the bottom of the cylinder. Punch holes in the top edge and add a yarn hanger. Ask your librarian to display the finished wind socks. Wind socks can also be made using holiday colors or theme-related pictures and sentences.

MONDAY

Reminders:_____

_____

_____

Notes:

TUESDAY

Reminders:_____

_____

_____

Notes:

WEDNESDAY

Reminders:_____

_____

_____

Notes:

THURSDAY

Reminders:_____

_____

_____

Notes:

FRIDAY

Reminders:_____

_____

_____

Notes:

THINK AND DO

Ask students to fashion a suitcase from 9'' x 12'' (23 cm x 30 cm) construction paper. Cut a 1/2'' (1.25 cm) strip from the 12'' (30 cm) side. Fold the remaining paper in half and cut and glue the strip to the top like a handle. Write the trip destination on the front of the suitcase and pack the bag by gluing pictures from clothing catalogs inside. Write a story about a real or make-believe trip. When reporting to the class, students may share travel brochures, maps, or photos. Younger students may pack a bag to take to grandma's or a friend's house for an overnight visit.

DAILY LESSON PLANS

MONDAY

Reminders: _____

_____

_____

Notes:

TUESDAY

Reminders: _____

_____

_____

Notes:

WEDNESDAY

Reminders: _____

_____

_____

Notes:

THURSDAY

Reminders: _____

_____

_____

Notes:

FRIDAY

Reminders: _____

_____

_____

Notes:

THINK AND DO

Home—Students can ask adults how they use math in their jobs. Show the students the connection between math and several careers. Discuss the importance of math skills in daily life: banking, sewing, cooking, construction, etc. Think about how other subjects like social studies, science, health, and reading are important to adults.

Discuss/write: What are you learning now in school that will help you as an adult? Why are interpersonal skills important? Why is it important to be on time and well-prepared every day?

MONDAY	Notes:				
Reminders: _____					

TUESDAY	Notes:				
Reminders: _____					

WEDNESDAY	Notes:				
Reminders: _____					

THURSDAY	Notes:				
Reminders: _____					

FRIDAY	Notes:				
Reminders: _____					

THINK AND DO

Arrange for your students to experience handicapping conditions by having them use blindfolds, ear plugs, or wheelchairs for a day. You may get these items on loan from a pharmacy that supplies hospital equipment.

Distribute reading samples without correct spacing and b, p, d reversals for deciphering. Here are some samples:

Doyourbesteverydayandyouwill be successful.

(Do your best every day and you will be successful).

The pig prown rappit hobbed pown the roap.

(The big brown rabbit hopped down the road).

DAILY LESSON PLANS

MONDAY

Reminders:_____

_____

_____

Notes:

TUESDAY

Reminders:_____

_____

_____

Notes:

WEDNESDAY

Reminders:_____

_____

_____

Notes:

THURSDAY

Reminders:_____

_____

_____

Notes:

FRIDAY

Reminders:_____

_____

_____

Notes:

THINK AND DO

Students will need to collect cardboard tubes, scissors, and masking tape. The tubes should be cut in half lengthwise to assemble a track. Students will need a marble or small toy car.

Have students experiment with track configurations that will allow the marble to move smoothly along the entire path or stop at a specific point. Use a stopwatch to time the travel of the marble and several different-sized cars. Students can brainstorm other things they can make from recycled items like foam meat trays, plastic two-liter bottles, cereal boxes, egg cartons, and fabric scraps.

MONDAY

Reminders: _____

_____

_____

Notes:

TUESDAY

Reminders: _____

_____

_____

Notes:

WEDNESDAY

Reminders: _____

_____

_____

Notes:

THURSDAY

Reminders: _____

_____

_____

Notes:

FRIDAY

Reminders: _____

_____

_____

Notes:

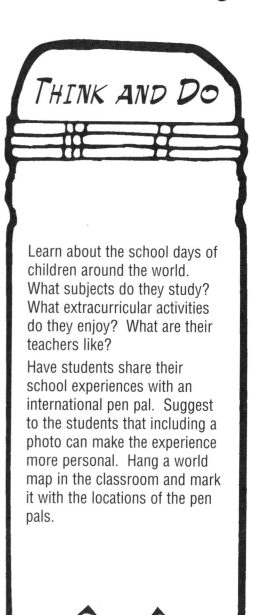

THINK AND DO

Learn about the school days of children around the world. What subjects do they study? What extracurricular activities do they enjoy? What are their teachers like?

Have students share their school experiences with an international pen pal. Suggest to the students that including a photo can make the experience more personal. Hang a world map in the classroom and mark it with the locations of the pen pals.

DAILY LESSON PLANS

MONDAY Reminders:_____ _____ _____	Notes:			
TUESDAY Reminders:_____ _____ _____	Notes:			
WEDNESDAY Reminders:_____ _____ _____	Notes:			
THURSDAY Reminders:_____ _____ _____	Notes:			
FRIDAY Reminders:_____ _____ _____	Notes:			

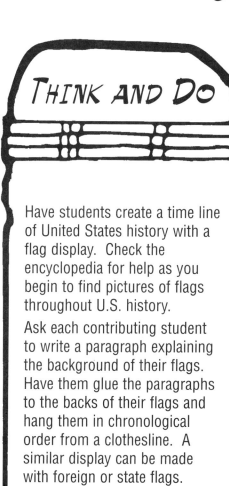

THINK AND DO

Have students create a time line of United States history with a flag display. Check the encyclopedia for help as you begin to find pictures of flags throughout U.S. history.

Ask each contributing student to write a paragraph explaining the background of their flags. Have them glue the paragraphs to the backs of their flags and hang them in chronological order from a clothesline. A similar display can be made with foreign or state flags.

Later, have students create a personal flag or one that represents their family or school.

MONDAY Reminders:_____ _____ _____	Notes:			
TUESDAY Reminders:_____ _____ _____	Notes:			
WEDNESDAY Reminders:_____ _____ _____	Notes:			
THURSDAY Reminders:_____ _____ _____	Notes:			
FRIDAY Reminders:_____ _____ _____	Notes:			

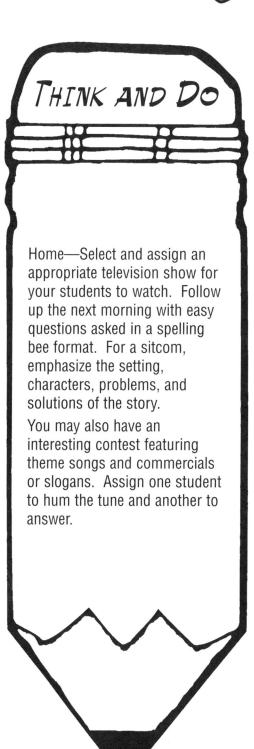

Think and Do

Home—Select and assign an appropriate television show for your students to watch. Follow up the next morning with easy questions asked in a spelling bee format. For a sitcom, emphasize the setting, characters, problems, and solutions of the story.

You may also have an interesting contest featuring theme songs and commercials or slogans. Assign one student to hum the tune and another to answer.

MONDAY

Reminders: _____

_____

_____

Notes:

TUESDAY

Reminders: _____

_____

_____

Notes:

WEDNESDAY

Reminders: _____

_____

_____

Notes:

THURSDAY

Reminders: _____

_____

_____

Notes:

FRIDAY

Reminders: _____

_____

_____

Notes:

THINK AND DO

Arrange a blind taste test of several brands of chocolate chip cookies, potato chips, bread, fruit drinks, etc. Include some samples of low fat, low sodium, and sugar free products. Ask students to rate their preferences (1–10) and write a critique, using adjectives to describe them. You will need 3–4 varieties of each item.

Blindfold the students while they are tasting. Make lists of foods that are sweet, sour, salty, and bitter.

Note: Check for any food allergies before beginning this activity.

WEEK OF_____ DAILY LESSON PLANS

MONDAY

Reminders:_____

_____

_____

Notes:

TUESDAY

Reminders:_____

_____

_____

Notes:

WEDNESDAY

Reminders:_____

_____

_____

Notes:

THURSDAY

Reminders:_____

_____

_____

Notes:

FRIDAY

Reminders:_____

_____

_____

Notes:

THINK AND DO

Home—Discuss with students how to find seeds in the foods they eat and in nature. Ask them to bring a variety of clean, dry seeds to class. Glue them to small tagboard squares with printed name labels. Sort the seeds by characteristics or category and put them in ABC order.

Soak and "plant" bean or corn seeds on several layers of damp paper toweling. They will sprout in 5–7 days if they are kept moist and in a lighted area.

Encourage students to begin collections of stamps, stickers, bottle caps, dolls, coins, etc. Invite those who have hobby collections to bring them to share with class members.

DAILY LESSON PLANS

MONDAY

Reminders:_____

_____

_____

Notes:

TUESDAY

Reminders:_____

_____

_____

Notes:

WEDNESDAY

Reminders:_____

_____

_____

Notes:

THURSDAY

Reminders:_____

_____

_____

Notes:

FRIDAY

Reminders:_____

_____

_____

Notes:

THINK AND DO

Home—Ask each child to bring a simple recipe from home. Trade the recipes and convert all measurements to metric. Prepare a center with rice and beans with cups and spoons for measuring practice.

Ask students to picture the foods on their recipe pages and compile a class cookbook. Gather a group of children's cookbooks for additional practice. Many of these will have sequential picture directions appropriate for nonreaders. If possible, select a recipe to prepare and enjoy at school. Rewrite a recipe in three clear sections: utensils, ingredients, and numbered directions.

MONDAY	Notes:			
Reminders:_____				
_____				
_____				

TUESDAY	Notes:			
Reminders:_____				
_____				
_____				

WEDNESDAY	Notes:			
Reminders:_____				
_____				
_____				

THURSDAY	Notes:			
Reminders:_____				
_____				
_____				

FRIDAY	Notes:			
Reminders:_____				
_____				
_____				

Think and Do

Trace and cut 30–40 child-sized footprints from colored tagboard. Space the footprints around the room to mark a game path. Secure them in place with masking tape loops. You may want to write directions on some of the footprints—like *lose one turn* or *move an extra space*. Make a large die by putting peel and press dots on a small box. Roll the die and have players move the corresponding number of steps along the path. The first player to reach the end is the winner. For a more difficult game, require each player to answer a skill question before progressing along the path.

WEEK OF_____ *DAILY LESSON PLANS*

MONDAY

Reminders:_____

_____

_____

Notes:

TUESDAY

Reminders:_____

_____

_____

Notes:

WEDNESDAY

Reminders:_____

_____

_____

Notes:

THURSDAY

Reminders:_____

_____

_____

Notes:

FRIDAY

Reminders:_____

_____

_____

Notes:

THINK AND DO

Have students make a toss/catch toy. Each student will need a paper towel roll, hole punch, scissors, 20 inches (50 cm) of string or yarn, and a plastic lid at least 6 inches (15 cm) in diameter. Cut the center out of the lid. Punch a hole in one end of the paper tube. Tie the tube and ring together with the length of yarn. Hold the tube with the ring hanging down. Move the tube and try to catch the ring. Students can try to guess how many times they will catch the ring in ten attempts.

MONDAY

Reminders:_____

_____

_____

Notes:

TUESDAY

Reminders:_____

_____

_____

Notes:

WEDNESDAY

Reminders:_____

_____

_____

Notes:

THURSDAY

Reminders:_____

_____

_____

Notes:

FRIDAY

Reminders:_____

_____

_____

Notes:

Think and Do

Have students look through magazines and catalogs for pictures of people wearing hats. Students will cut and glue them onto a chart into two categories: occupation and decoration. At the end of the week, have Hat Day with each child wearing a special hat. If necessary, provide supplies for children to make hats. You may do similar projects for shoes. Cut catalog pictures and sort them: men's, women's, children's. Print labels: boots, slippers, high heels, athletic, etc., for matching. Ask students to create (on paper) a shoe to serve a special purpose. Write a paragraph to explain its use.

MONDAY	Notes:			
Reminders:_____				
_____				
_____				

TUESDAY	Notes:			
Reminders:_____				
_____				
_____				

WEDNESDAY	Notes:			
Reminders:_____				
_____				
_____				

THURSDAY	Notes:			
Reminders:_____				
_____				
_____				

FRIDAY	Notes:			
Reminders:_____				
_____				
_____				

Think and Do

Draw a detailed diagram of your classroom. Label the desks with the students' names. Have the class work in groups to draw a map of the path from your classroom to the cafeteria, auditorium, library, or playground.

Older students may make maps showing their paths from home to school, including houses, parks, stores, and public buildings. Have the students look at city maps to locate specific streets and intersections. Suggest using the telephone book to find addresses for the library, police station, grocery store, etc. Mark them on the maps.

DAILY LESSON PLANS

MONDAY

Reminders:_____

_____

_____

Notes:				

TUESDAY

Reminders:_____

_____

_____

Notes:				

WEDNESDAY

Reminders:_____

_____

_____

Notes:				

THURSDAY

Reminders:_____

_____

_____

Notes:				

FRIDAY

Reminders:_____

_____

_____

Notes:				

THINK AND DO

Brainstorm with the class a list of things they can do with a recycled paper (or foam) cup. Provide art supplies and have children make samples of some of the ideas.

Bring soil and bean seeds for planting. Have students poke a small hole in the bottom of their cups. Each student should cover the seeds with soil and water and place the cup in a sunny window.

Discuss the problem of over crowding in our landfills and encourage your students to avoid excessive use of paper products. Encourage your students to recycle at home and challenge them to look for ways to limit the use of paper products in school offices, classrooms, and cafeteria.

MONDAY	Notes:				
Reminders:_____					
_____					
_____					

TUESDAY	Notes:				
Reminders:_____					
_____					
_____					

WEDNESDAY	Notes:				
Reminders:_____					
_____					
_____					

THURSDAY	Notes:				
Reminders:_____					
_____					
_____					

FRIDAY	Notes:				
Reminders:_____					
_____					
_____					

THINK AND DO

Have each student think of a famous person whom they admire. Have them explain why they feel as they do and what it might be like to have that person for a friend. Have students research information and prepare a brief report. Suggest to the students that they dress like their hero while they deliver their report in the first person. Suggest having props (athletic gear, concert programs, etc.) or preparing a class activity relating to the person. Compile a class list of heroes and plan additional experiences around these role models. You may find videos, recordings, or books to use as extensions.

DAILY LESSON PLANS

MONEY	Notes:			
MONDAY				
Reminders:				
TUESDAY	Notes:			
Reminders:				
WEDNESDAY	Notes:			
Reminders:				
THURSDAY	Notes:			
Reminders:				
FRIDAY	Notes:			
Reminders:				

THINK AND DO

Home—Have students think of as many ways as they can to entertain their family without spending money or relying on electronic media. Examples you can give the children are playing board games, reading, gardening, cooking, crafts, etc. Have the students explain why each activity is appropriate for different family members. After the students try out their ideas, have them report the results to the class. Extend the project by researching how early Americans spent their free time. Arrange for students to experience activities like playing checkers, making their own toys, quilting, etc. Discuss the pros and cons of past and present life styles.

WEEK OF_____ DAILY LESSON PLANS

MONDAY

Reminders:_____

_____

_____

Notes:

TUESDAY

Reminders:_____

_____

_____

Notes:

WEDNESDAY

Reminders:_____

_____

_____

Notes:

THURSDAY

Reminders:_____

_____

_____

Notes:

FRIDAY

Reminders:_____

_____

_____

Notes:

THINK AND DO

Students can design souvenirs that can be sold to promote their hometown. Brainstorm with the children ideas about what makes the place where they live special. Have students make drawings and write descriptions of the items. In groups, have students decide on prices and marketing plans. A newspaper advertisement can be created to show all the necessary information. Have the students trade their ideas and drawings with other class members and ask them to write a critique of each souvenir. Is it worth the price? Does it promote the area? Do you think many people would buy it? How might it be improved? Explain.

DAILY LESSON PLANS

MONDAY

Reminders: _____

_____

_____

Notes:

TUESDAY

Reminders: _____

_____

_____

Notes:

WEDNESDAY

Reminders: _____

_____

_____

Notes:

THURSDAY

Reminders: _____

_____

_____

Notes:

FRIDAY

Reminders: _____

_____

_____

Notes:

THINK AND DO

Have students make this friendship bracelet: Precut ¹/₂'' x 2'' (1.25 cm x 5 cm) strips of lightweight tagboard for each student. Students will print their names on one strip and their best friends' names on the other. Punch holes in both ends of the name cards and tie them together with colored ribbon or yarn bows. Students can share the bracelet with the friend whose name is on it.

Discuss what qualities make someone a good friend. Have students cut a string of paper dolls and write a friend's name on each one. Add colorful details and let students display them from the edges of their desks.

DAILY LESSON PLANS

MONDAY

Reminders:_____

_____

_____

Notes:

TUESDAY

Reminders:_____

_____

_____

Notes:

WEDNESDAY

Reminders:_____

_____

_____

Notes:

THURSDAY

Reminders:_____

_____

_____

Notes:

FRIDAY

Reminders:_____

_____

_____

Notes:

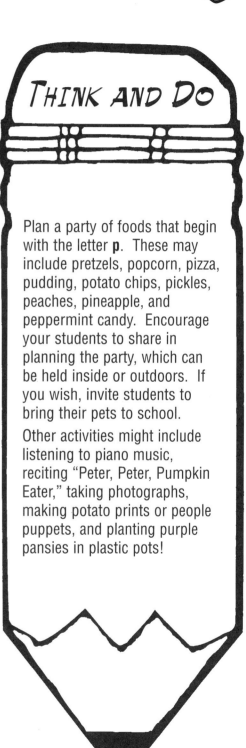

Think and Do

Plan a party of foods that begin with the letter **p**. These may include pretzels, popcorn, pizza, pudding, potato chips, pickles, peaches, pineapple, and peppermint candy. Encourage your students to share in planning the party, which can be held inside or outdoors. If you wish, invite students to bring their pets to school.

Other activities might include listening to piano music, reciting "Peter, Peter, Pumpkin Eater," taking photographs, making potato prints or people puppets, and planting purple pansies in plastic pots!

MONDAY

Reminders:_____

_____

_____

Notes:

TUESDAY

Reminders:_____

_____

_____

Notes:

WEDNESDAY

Reminders:_____

_____

_____

Notes:

THURSDAY

Reminders:_____

_____

_____

Notes:

FRIDAY

Reminders:_____

_____

_____

Notes:

THINK AND DO

Brainstorm with the class a list of careers. Have the children choose their favorite. Have each student write a riddle with three clues ending with "Who am I?" Ask students to draw a picture of the worker. Combine all the pages in a class book. Have students learn more about the job of an adult they know. Suggest drawing a picture of that person working. A great way for the student to experience that job is to accompany the adult to work for a day. Make a Venn diagram comparing two different jobs. Which one is best? Which one is worst? Explain your choice. Make webs for each career, showing tools, uniform, working conditions, and necessary training. Encourage students to begin making decisions about what they might like to be in the future.

DAILY LESSON PLANS

MONDAY

Reminders:_____

_____

_____

Notes:

TUESDAY

Reminders:_____

_____

_____

Notes:

WEDNESDAY

Reminders:_____

_____

_____

Notes:

THURSDAY

Reminders:_____

_____

_____

Notes:

FRIDAY

Reminders:_____

_____

_____

Notes:

THINK AND DO

Prepare a word scavenger hunt, directing students to find specific words in a reading sample or newspaper page. Here are some things for which they might search: a color word, a number word, a proper name, a word ending with -ing, a word ending in -ed, a place, a person, an animal, a word beginning with th-, and a word beginning with wh-. Look for appropriate grade level words. Cut and glue several words to form sentences. Older students may cut and paste words for three clues, explaining how to solve a mystery (find a hidden object or name a specific person).

DAILY LESSON PLANS

MONDAY

Reminders: _____

_____

_____

Notes:

TUESDAY

Reminders: _____

_____

_____

Notes:

WEDNESDAY

Reminders: _____

_____

_____

Notes:

THURSDAY

Reminders: _____

_____

_____

Notes:

FRIDAY

Reminders: _____

_____

_____

Notes:

THINK AND DO

Have students make tube characters to complement any theme unit. Children can use their creativity and imaginations to design freestanding animals and/or people. The materials are inexpensive and readily available. Provide the following: construction paper, glue, markers, stapler, scissors, and cardboard tubes. Design a character and color and cut it out. Staple a three-inch (8 cm) length of tube at the bottom or cut a slit in the tube and insert the drawing so that it will be freestanding. Use the characters for a display of family members, storybook characters, zoo animals, or an original puppet show.

DAILY LESSON PLANS

MONDAY

Reminders:_____

_____

_____

Notes:

TUESDAY

Reminders:_____

_____

_____

Notes:

WEDNESDAY

Reminders:_____

_____

_____

Notes:

THURSDAY

Reminders:_____

_____

_____

Notes:

FRIDAY

Reminders:_____

_____

_____

Notes:

90

THINK AND DO

Home—Ask each student to bring several clean, empty product packages from home in a brown paper bag (so they cannot be seen). On arriving at school, students will trade bags and write a story which includes all the items in the new bag. Have the class share their stories and show the items. Later use the packages in a classroom store. Assign prices and practice counting money and making change. Ask the students to order the items in ABC order, classify them, or practice using a calculator for series addition. Younger children may listen and respond to directions like "Give me two cereals and a cake mix." or "I'd like a pizza and a bottle of soda."

WEEK OF _____ DAILY LESSON PLANS

MONDAY Reminders:_____ _____ _____	Notes:				
TUESDAY Reminders:_____ _____ _____	Notes:				
WEDNESDAY Reminders:_____ _____ _____	Notes:				
THURSDAY Reminders:_____ _____ _____	Notes:				
FRIDAY Reminders:_____ _____ _____	Notes:				

THINK AND DO

You will need dice, a marker, and a blank piece of half-inch (1.25 cm) graph paper for this activity. On the paper create a graph with the numbers 2–12 across the bottom and 1–25 up the left-hand side. Each student will roll the dice one time and chart their totals by coloring one square on the graph. Before you begin, ask students to guess which number will occur most frequently and write it down. After the activity, ask students to determine why some numbers occur more often than others (they have more possible combinations). Young children may make the graph using only one die.

WEEK OF _____ DAILY LESSON PLANS

MONDAY

Reminders:_____

_____

_____

Notes:

TUESDAY

Reminders:_____

_____

_____

Notes:

WEDNESDAY

Reminders:_____

_____

_____

Notes:

THURSDAY

Reminders:_____

_____

_____

Notes:

FRIDAY

Reminders:_____

_____

_____

Notes:

THINK AND DO

Gather and share a collection of alphabet books. Invite young children to shape their bodies like letters or arrange a group of children into a specific letter shape. Have students highlight letters in newspaper headlines. Cut letter shapes from sandpaper or sponges for painting. Allow students to "print" letters in trays of salt, sand, or flour. Show an array of letter cards in ABC order and ask which comes before or after or give the students groups of random cards to sequence. Brainstorm a list of nouns for each consonant and write original tongue-twister sentences. Older students may make alphabet books to share with younger grades.

NOTES